30119 023 986 492

D1758644

Mel Bay Presents

TANGOS & MILONGAS
For Solo Guitar

by Jorge Morel

CD CONTENTS

1	Milonga del Viento [3:20]
2	Otro Tango, Buenos Aires [3:53]
3	El Choclo [2:45]
4	Gallo Ciego [3:18]
5	Don Agustin Bardi [2:51]

1 2 3 4 5 6 7 8 9 0

Visit us on the Web at http://www.melbay.com — E-mail us at email@melbay.com

About the Author

Jorge Morel, born in Argentina and now living and working in New York City, has performed for thousands of international audiences in the last three decades incorporating brilliant technique, a uniquely personal style and sophisticated artistic expression. As impressive as his record as a performing artist is, Morel's creative contributions as a composer have achieved the respect and recognition of his peers and established his position as a leader in the ongoing development of the classical guitar.

Contents

Don Agustin Bardi 4

Gallo Ciego 13

El Choclo 24

Milonga del Viento 29

Otro Tango, Buenos Aires 36

Horacia Salgan, one of Argentina's leading composer-pianists and a great master of the tango, composed this magnificent piece dedicated to another great composer, Agustin Bardi.

Don Agustin Bardi

Horacio Salgan
Arr. Jorge Morel

4

CODA

Don Agustin Bardi

Horacio Salgan
Arr. Jorge Morel

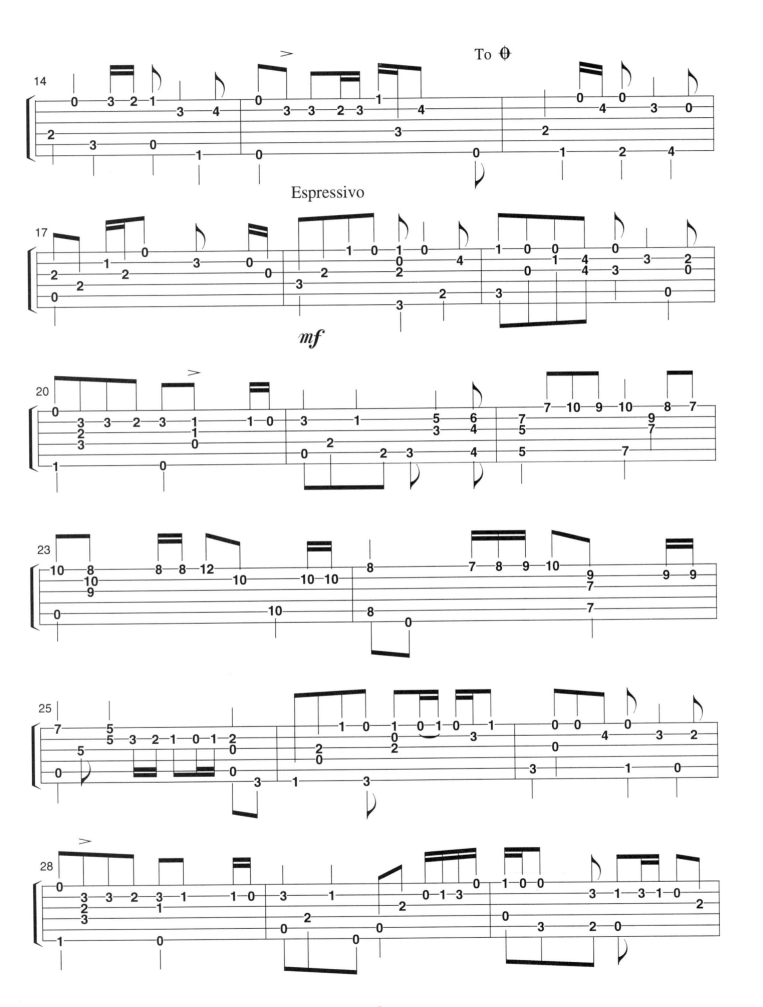

a tempo

Har.

f

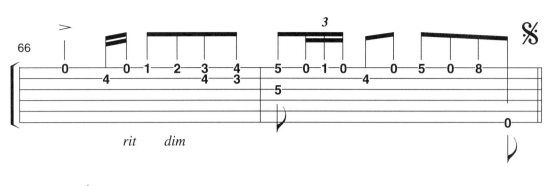

rit   dim

CODA

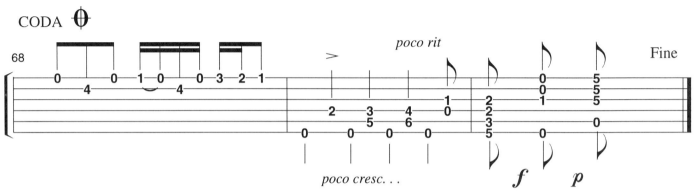

poco cresc. . .

poco rit

f   *p*

Fine

Composed by Agustin Bardi for small orchestra, more than 50 years ago, *Gallo Ciego* is still one of the most performed tangos in the country and perhaps the favorite of most tango dancers.

Gallo Ciego

Agustin Bardi
Arr. Jorge Morel

Allegretto Moderato

Gallo Ciego
Tango

Agustin Bardi
Arr. Jorge Morel

Allegretto Moderato

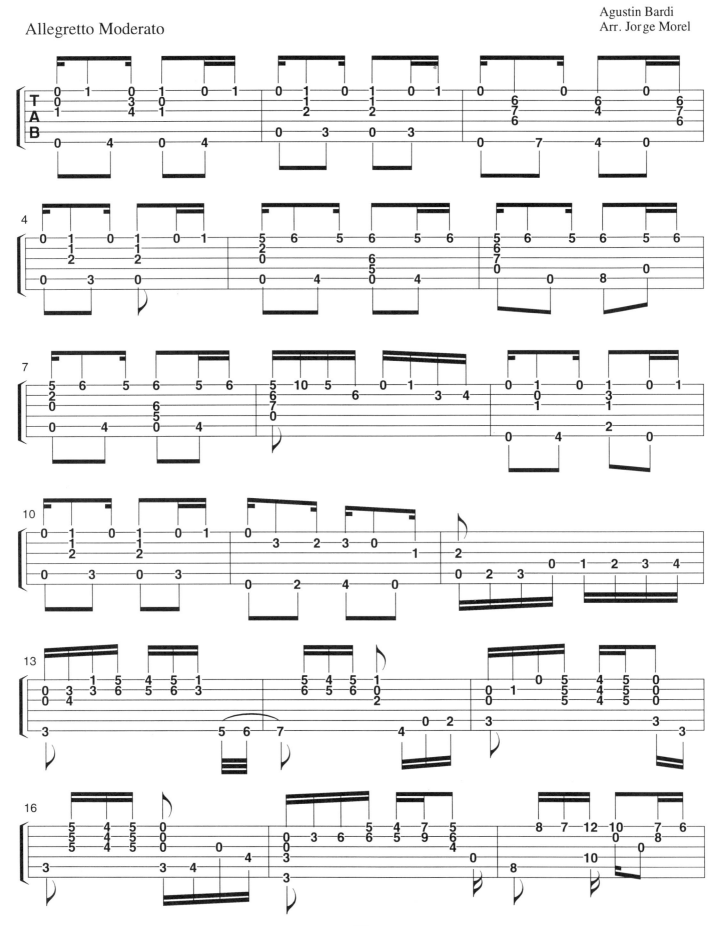

Espressivo

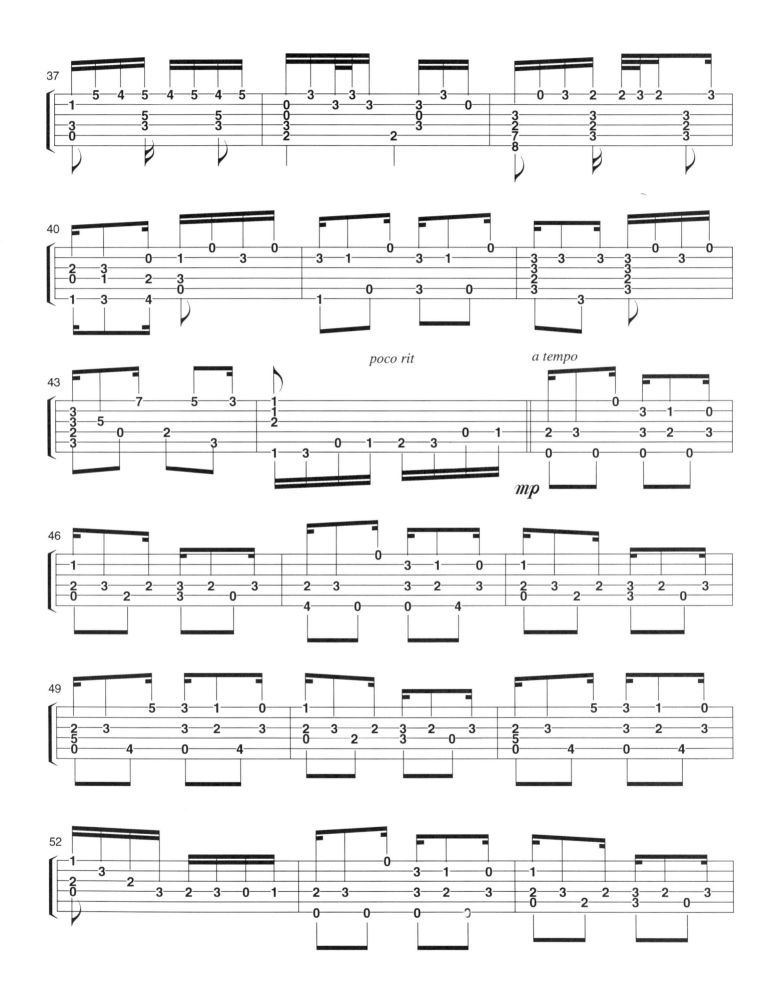

poco rit   a tempo

mp

20

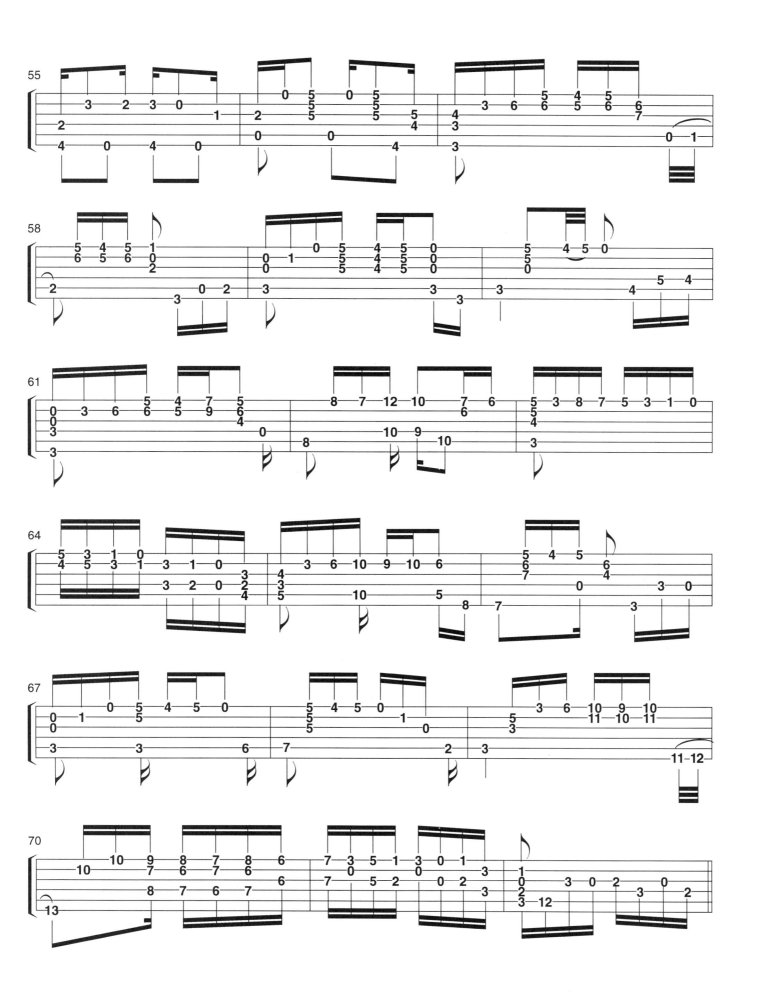

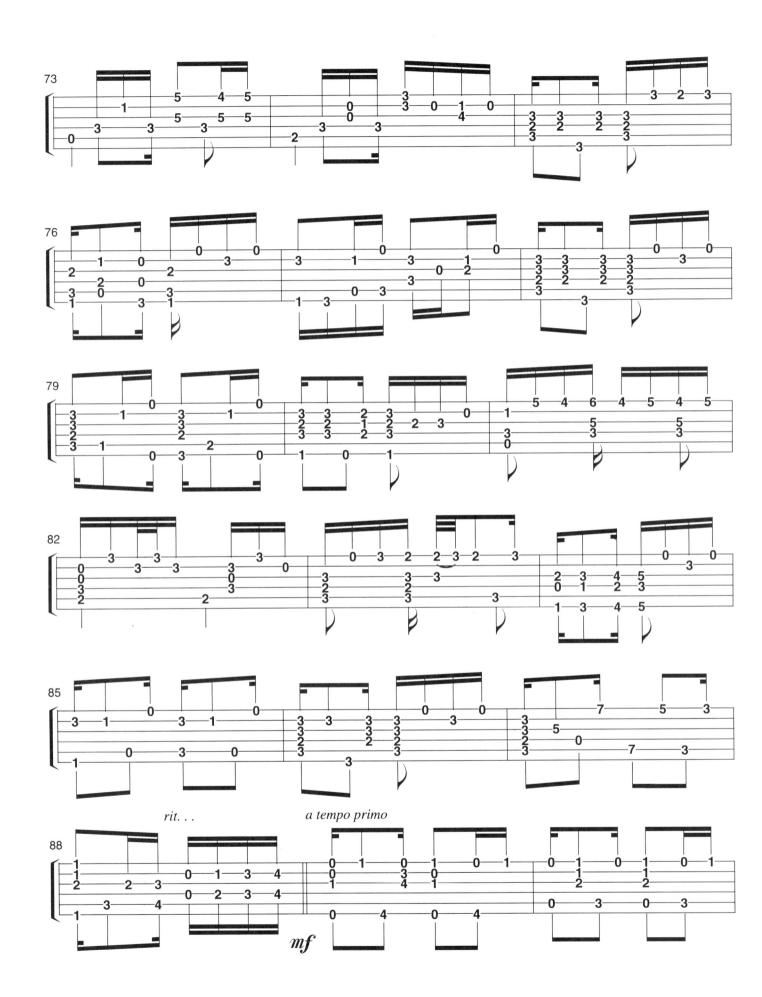

rit. . .

a tempo primo

mf

22

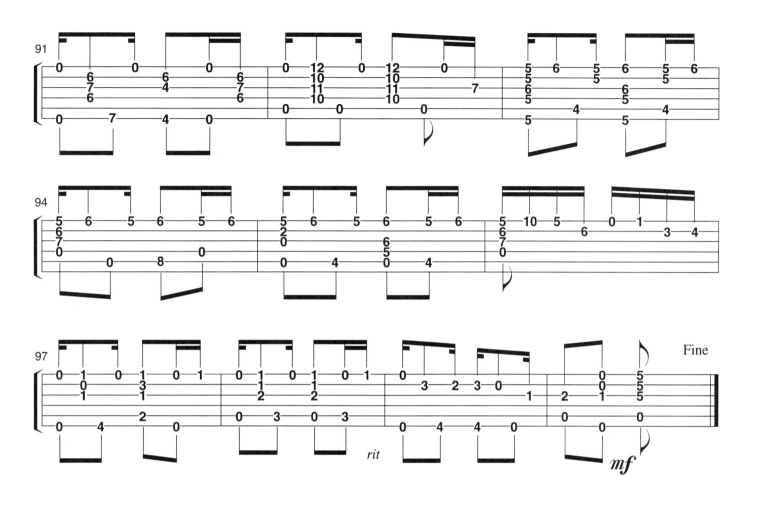

El Choclo is one of the most popular and loved tangos in Argentina. Its rhythm is also combined with that of the milonga, so it may be called tango-milonga.

El Choclo

Angel Villoldo
Arr. Jorge Morel

Har.   Har.

CODA ⊕

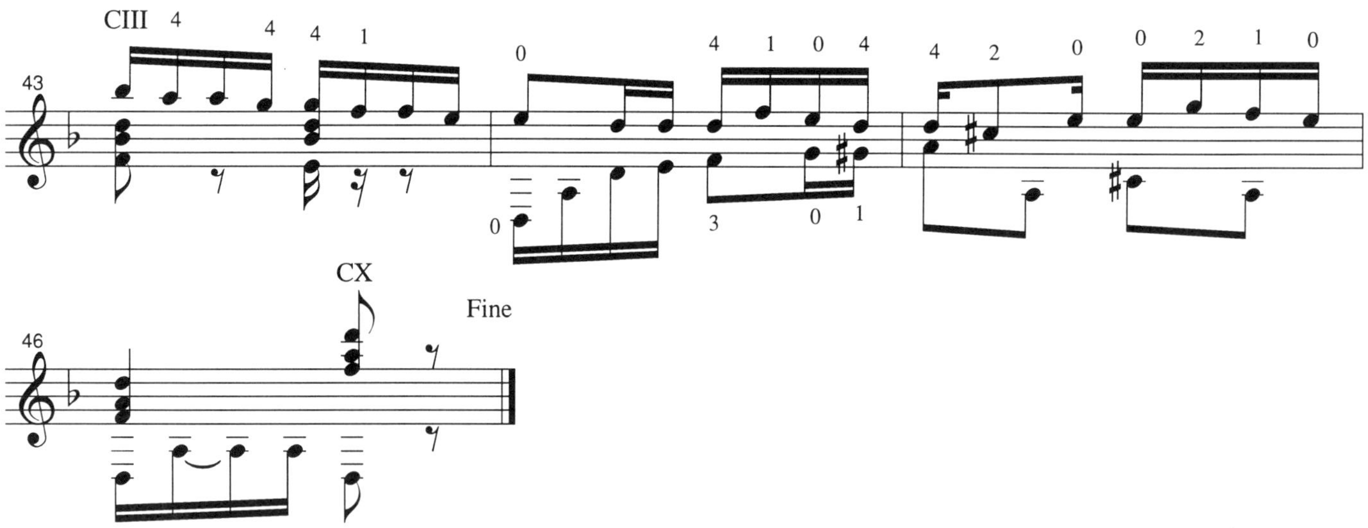

El Choclo

Angel Villoldo
Arr. Jorge Morel

There are two types of milongas in Argentina. One is of slow tempo like this one and the other is a bit faster; both are written in 2/4 time. In this piece I use the traditional bass line of 3-3 plus 2, 16th notes, that give the work a real feeling of the dance.

Milonga del Viento

Jorge Morel

Milonga del Viento

Moderato

Jorge Morel

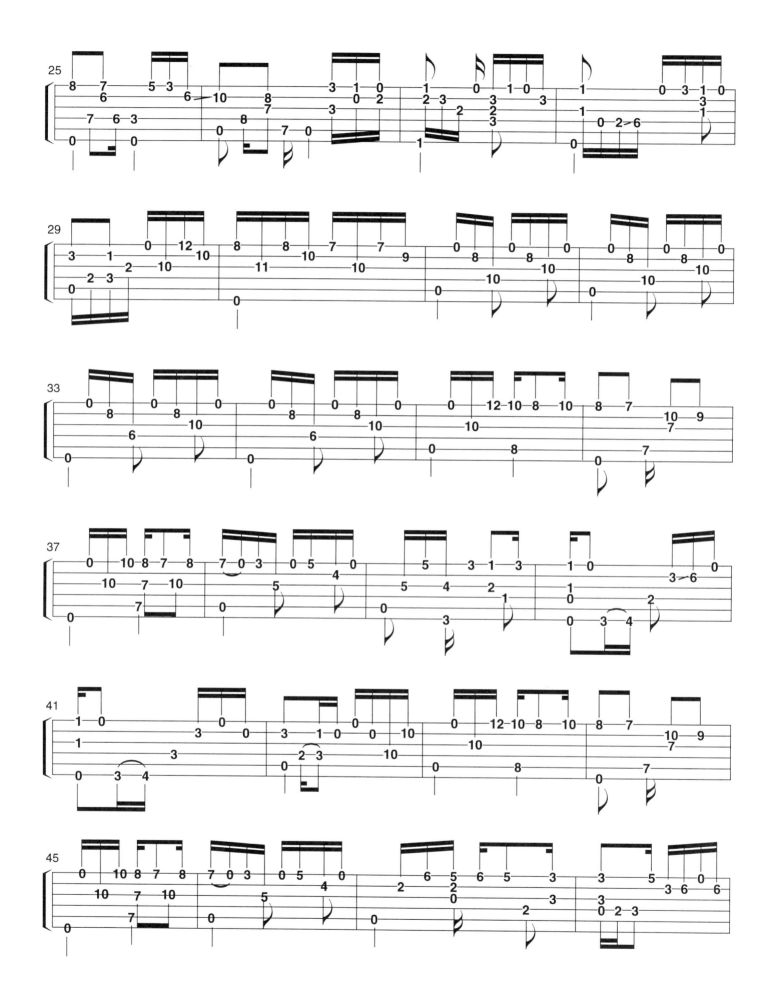

molto rit

mp

Fine

35

This is an arrangement for solo guitar from excerpts of Rapsodia Del Sur, a composition I wrote for guitar and string orchestra in 1996 in memory of my brother. This is part of the second movement that is mostly tango rhythm.

Otro Tango, Buenos Aires
(In Memory of my Brother)
From Rapsodia Del Sur

Jorge Morel

Otro Tango, Buenos Aires

(In Memory of my Brother)
From *Rapsodia Del Sur*

Jorge Morel

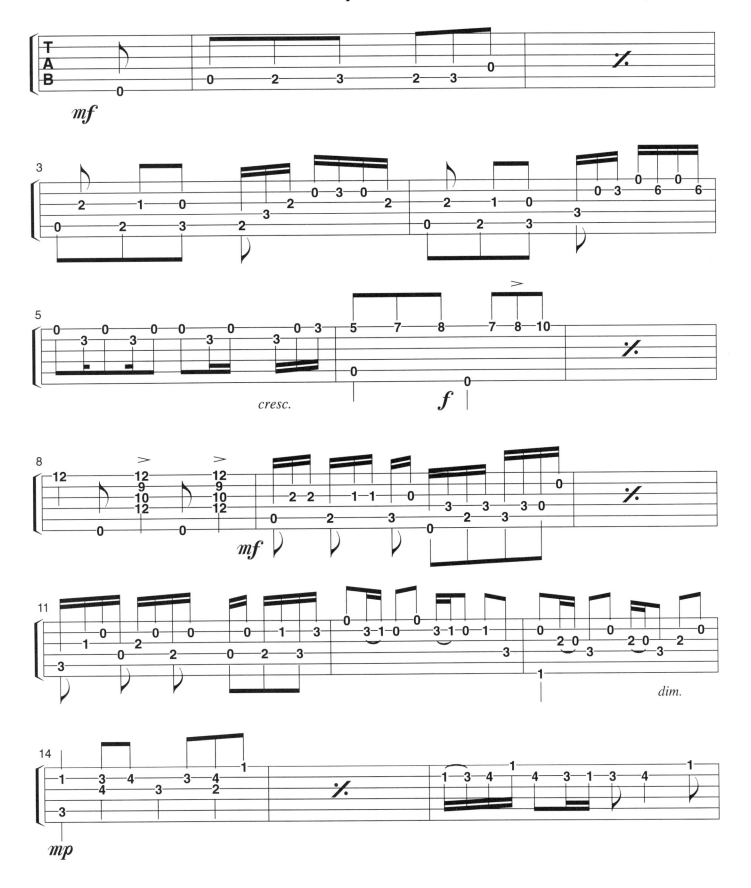

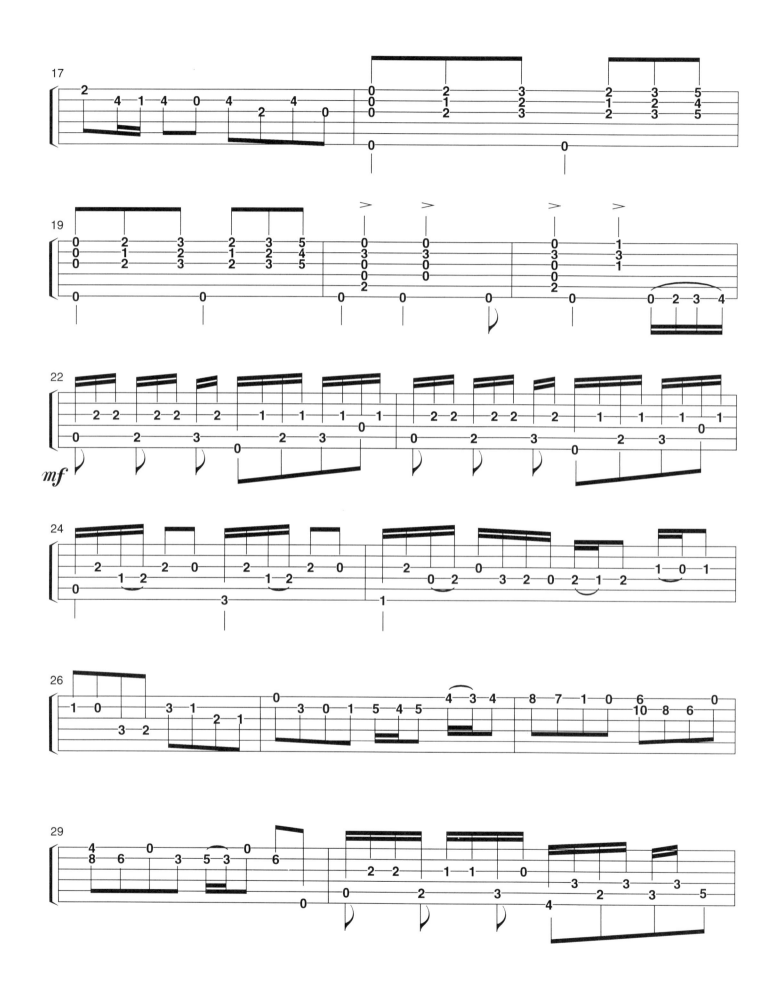

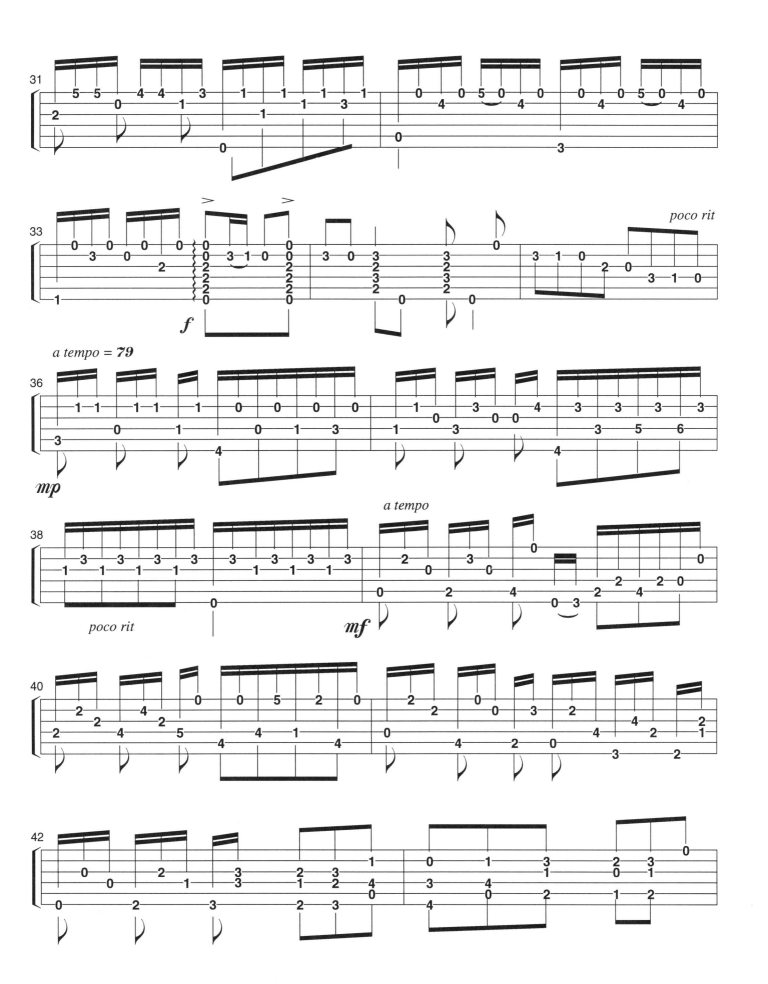

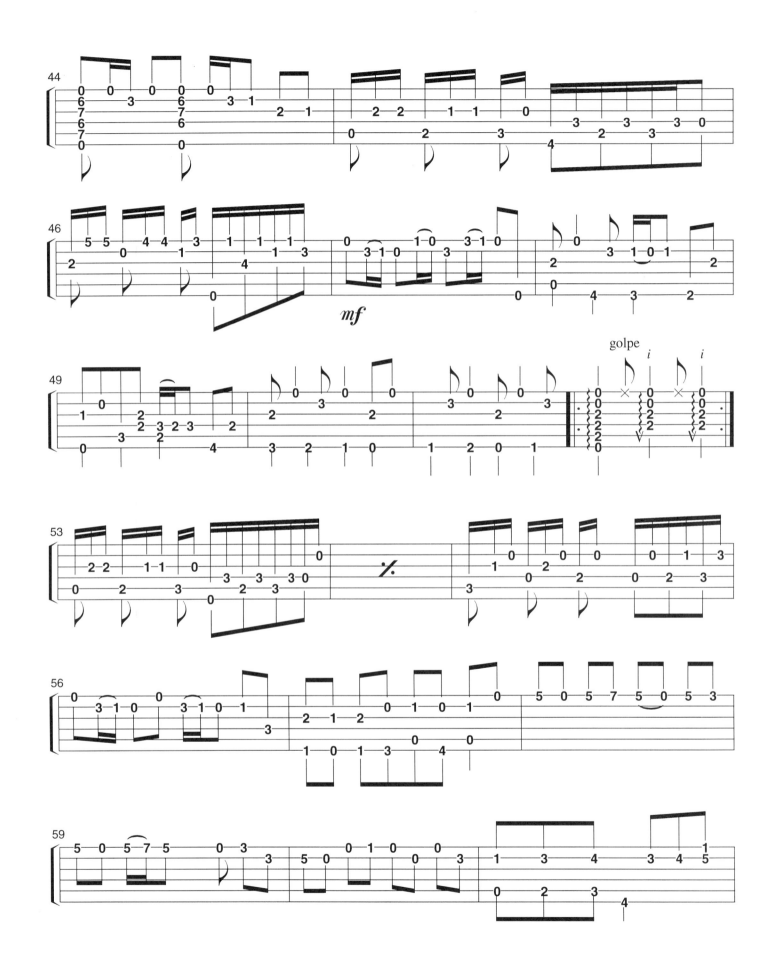

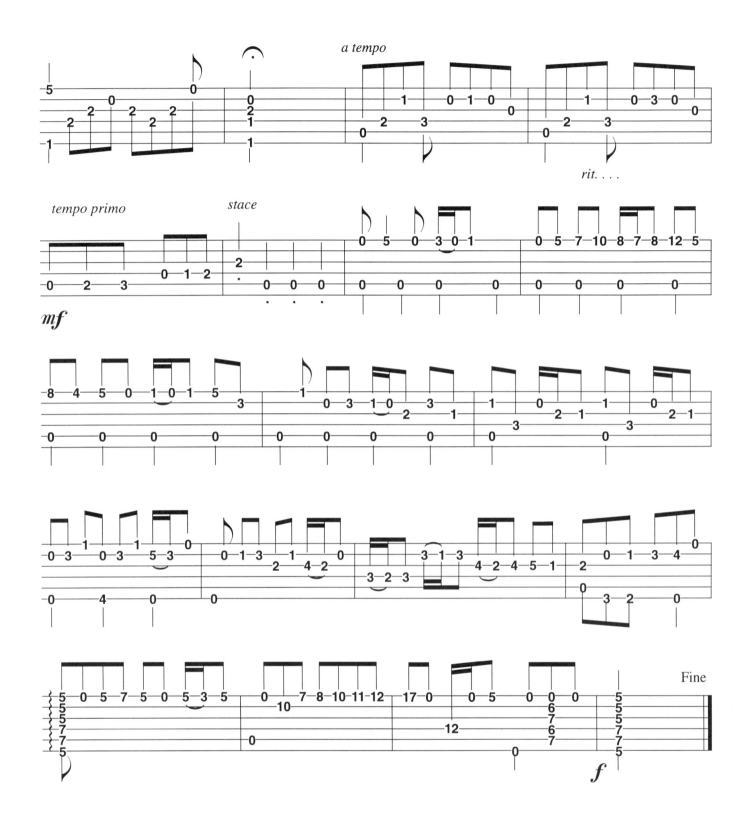